T0196300

JUMPER CABLES

JUMPER CABLES

JUMPSTART YOUR LIFE AND CAREER BATTERY TO NEW LEVELS OF SUCCESS

BY: W. TIM DODD

authorHOUSE®

AuthorHouse™ LLC
1663 Liberty Drive
Bloomington, IN 47403
www.authorhouse.com
Phone: 1-800-839-8640

Published by AuthorHouse   08/07/2013

ISBN: 978-1-4772-9739-1 (sc)
ISBN: 978-1-4772-9738-4 (e)

Library of Congress Control Number: 2012923204

Message from the author

Jumper Cables and its use is a symbolic illustration of my professional and personal journey. It is a sharing of the disabilities and obstacles I have confronted and overcome. I have encountered numerous experiences in life, many may be similar to yours. In my opinion, experiences offer a tremendous purpose—the opportunity to learn and grow. Key experiences are meant to be shared in order not to repeat history. I offer these not to brag or complain, rather to offer insight in order to help others not repeat the same lessons learned.

Throughout the following pages of this book, many references will be made to the destination or goal that was being pursued. The key learning for me was that the destination ended being a new beginning—meaning, there was no ending. The experiences shared in the following pages were learning opportunities along the journey. When each was embraced, growth occurred. It does not mean the destination always turned out as planned or envisioned; rather, it offered a perspective that was broader in scope than when first considered.

Life offers disabilities and obstacles to everyone. Jumper Cables, the right help at the right time, is about not becoming a victim but to confront and challenge the disabilities and obstacles. It is about an attitude of continuous improving of self with determination and commitment. Filtered throughout this book are many references to my main source of strength—my faith. It is the core of who and why I am who I am. For you the reader, your source may come from other spheres. That's okay, just understand the theme and connect to your source. My reference to my faith is not meant to offend, but to identify my source of strength.

Jumper Cables is sharing the journey of my career and experiences and how I stayed true to my faith, family, professional commitment, values, and self. My hope is that Jumper Cables can help motivate you to connect with your reliable source of strength and begin your journey to that desired destination.

This book is dedicated to my wife, Diana, of thirty-seven years. She has stood beside me though the journeys described in this book and so many others. Her continued love and support continues to be my source of motivation to continually improve and be the best I can possibly be.

Thank you and recognition to several who helped make this book possible:

Dr. Martha J. Cook, Editor and author of Grammar toward Professionals

Dr. David Watterson, Watterson and Associates Inc., whose coaching and mentoring has been a key source in my professional development and success.

Gideon Oswitch, Human Resource Generalist and Author, whose encouragement and writing style inspired me to complete this book.

Robert Karras, R.Karras Asset Management & Planning, LLC, Cleveland, Ohio, my very close friend who has become more than a brother to me that continually inspires me to keep pursuing all my goals in life.

My wife Diana, who has been forever my greatest fan and cheerleader giving me the support and confidence to write this book along with being by my side through this entire journey.

My daughters, Michelle and Megan, whom in their journey to becoming incredible successful young women has inspired me to continue reaching for goals that I never thought possible.

Introduction

"All the strength and force of man comes from his faith in things unseen. He who believes is strong; he who doubts is weak. Strong convictions precede great actions."

J.F. Clarke

Jumper Cables . . . Go ahead and ping-pong that item in your head and what comes to mind? If, as I do, you envision an essential part of a car's emergency pack stowed away in a dirty corner of your car's trunk, this will take on a parallel meaning as I explain. Jumper cables are not too expensive and most drivers have been tutored *ad infinitum* to always have a pair of these in the car at all times just in case the battery is dead or is having the last rites administered as the key is turned (always at a very inopportune time) and hear that sickening click—click—click sound. When that does transpire, attach the cables to a fresh, stronger battery of another car and tap into the power supply to get that battery kick started. Caution must be exercised—if the cables are improperly connected, the good battery can arc out and possibly do irreparable damage to the car's electrical system.

Keep in mind that if the battery is new, always charged and well maintained, then guess what? One may never need the cables to jump start a battery, but one may be called upon to help someone whom you happen to see in need. Pretty simple concept; nothing too complex.

Or is it?

Take a second to examine where you are in life. Is your battery getting low—needs recharged? How is your career? Are you happy with decisions you have made in life? What about regrets you have encountered? How strong are your devoted relationships to your family? What about your commitment to faith? Your dedication to your country? Are you happy with yourself; personal appearance; intelligence? Do you really feel fulfilled? These are very difficult questions that people tend to ignore as they live their day-to-day events. Then one day a person wakes up and to realize that they are not who or where they want to be in life; via a battery malfunctioned. The battery stopped working and the "help" wasn't there.

If you are in the minority who is perfectly satisfied with life, then put this book down and get your derriere outside and help someone with whom fate purposely put in your path. If you are the majority, do you feel a staleness professionally, a void with your family and spiritual relationships, or just feel like a battery whose energy indicator is tilting towards zero charge? If so, then this book is your rejuvenator. I can help you find success through my experiences in life, my hardships, interactions with other cultures, my corporate collaborations and decisions, and my deep down devotion to family and faith. Through my knowledge base and my quest to never be totally satisfied in whatever endeavor I actively pursue, I may be able to help you achieve your goals (and with that, happiness will not be far behind). As the title implies, this book is your jumper cable to achieving success, overcoming obstacles (whether you visualize them or not) and reaching a desired destination. You may have many "cables"; use them wisely. Sometimes in life we just need a little boost—to quote Bruce Springsteen, "You can't start a fire without a spark." So what is the energy to which you can connect your jumper cables for that spark? I hope this book gives you a motivational spark, a renewed desire towards success, a jumpstart to a new—mid-ending career, a planned-out schematic boost to achieving a goal that you have subconsciously believed you could attain. You are taking the first step by reading this book—now connect the dots in the following chapters and allow me to offer you some fresh enthusiasm, an energized charge and burst of power into your life's battery. Remember, when properly applied, to a potentially viable source, jumper cables always work! You just need to allow them to be correctly connected to your workable source and use your battery already in place. That's where this book will help identify problems, offer reliable help, and solutions. However keep the cables!

CHAPTER 1

"Coach, I can't run that play."
"Why"?
"Because it is not in the play book—we have never done it before."
"Then go find a better playbook."

It is another sultry June in northeast Ohio—as most folks are planning their Father's Day celebrations, I am sitting on the tarmac at Hopkins Airport in Cleveland, Ohio, with a few of my company's peers preparing to leave for China. Did I just say, "China"? Is this really happening? What am I doing sitting on this airplane en route to Asia? I never asked for this assignment—in fact, I was 99 percent dead set against my company's expanding towards the Pacific Rim; I knew this was an emerging market and there were strong sales opportunities, but I always needed to keep all manufacturing jobs in the USA, and more specifically, in northeast Ohio. To digress, a few days earlier, my supervisor called me into his office after a staff meeting and we had a conversation that I need to paraphrase:

"Tim, I am looking for someone to lead the China Project."

"Really? How is that going"?

"It is going well right now; I've made my decision and it's you. I have mentally begun the process to find your replacement for your current job."

Hmmm. Not much time for me to curl up in a ball and start screaming the way my grand daughter used to do around her first birthday if she did not get her own way. Instead, I quickly composed myself and tried to hide the utter panic that was percolating at spillover boil in my mind—China? This is a communist country where I know no one, don't speak the language, don't know the culture, and have heard numerous horror stories about traveling there. There probably was not another director in all my company more petrified (or against this proposition) than I to go to China and, according to my supervisor, I was going to be leading a project to set up contact points, meet contractors, and help build a new facility. No pressure at all! Here I was, the person least wanting to go and now being hand-selected to lead an extremely important start-up project. Ironically but not humorously, it reminded me of the story of the person who invented the guillotine; it then was then used to chop off his head! The plane hasn't even backed out of the gate yet and I am already getting air sickness . . . .

When I told my wife this news, she was not too pleased—our two daughters had moved to their own living quarters and we had begun to enjoy each other's company in the evenings—this was going to upset that happy family apple cart, and I knew would cause my wife to get nervous because of my being in a foreign country. This only added fuel to my worry-o-meter and as the plane took off; I started rethinking through everything that brought me to this point in time. I guess the Company must have a ton of faith in my abilities or the company would not have picked me, right? I take that as a positive spin on things, though I am still asking, "why me?" Why am I not going on a long exotic vacation with my wife? That would have made more sense. The closest I have ever been to China was eating lunches at Chinese restaurants close to our manufacturing plant and something is misconceptionally telling me that the country, China, is not going to be as clean, polite, less crowded and tasty as the Asian diner in Ohio. It is also going to be more than 10 minutes from my office. But at this point, I know that if I want to keep my job of 30 years with my company, one learns to nod his head when these special assignments are handed down—not much different from little league when the pitcher hits two consecutive batters in the head and the coach yells down the bench, "Dodd, you are going to pinch hit for O'Malley; grab some lumber and don't be scared." Both situations made me scared of the unknown. You see, I don't gamble; I like to control my atmosphere and this trip was throwing an enormous curve ball in my realm of control and I have never liked that feeling. To help gain some advantage for this trip, I took a four hour cultural class through the company to help gain a better understanding of China—that was very helpful, but was still only a four hour class.

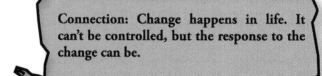

Connection: Change happens in life. It can't be controlled, but the response to the change can be.

Hours later, it is night time and the plane is quietly humming over the North Pole; most of the passengers are sleeping, but I am wide eyed due to a recent antihistamine which has not yet decided to do its job, I erratically am thinking about my daughters, thinking about my wife, thinking about my deceased father (who would have been pretty proud of me right now), thinking about my mom and imagine her telling her friends about her son's flying to China, thinking about my 23 year old sister, Becky, who for whatever reason, was taken away too young almost 30 years ago, and I am thinking about the twists and turns my career took to get me to this moment suspended in space 30,000 feet above the ground. I looked out the window at blackness, closed my eyes, and for some reason, "Does Anybody Really Know What Time It Is?" by the musical group Chicago popped into my head. I started humming it a bit, and the words caught me off guard:

> Don't know where I am
> Can't see past the next step
> Don't have the time to think past the last mile
> Have no time to look around
> Just run around, run around and think why.

The antihistamine must have hit full stride right at that moment because the next thing I recall was the pilot announcing our initial approach into China. Wow, that went quicker than I thought—time to clear my head, put on my business appearance and grab the playbook; my company was depending on me.

"Wish I didn't know now, what I didn't know then."
—Bob Seger

Fear is a pretty powerful emotion; it may become the best motivator. Fear usually makes its host pay a hundred percent full attention when it kicks into action (just watch my wife move when a snake scurries by her in the backyard!). Conventional wisdom tells us to face our fears, though most of us would rather avoid them. And now for me, I was facing a gargantuan fear at night in a hotel room in Taiwan before our trip to China. The room was clean, neat and reminiscent of a Hampton Inn style room. It definitely had that sterile feeling to it, though my mood made it seem more like hotel illness. Anyway, I was hoping to stretch out, relax and spend some well-earned time talking to my wife. Alas, the phone gremlins were coughing up a fur ball as I could not get an international signal back to the US and my cell phone was lacking any type of US-domestic reception. At this point, one could add being severely agitated as an additional seasoning to my fearful frustration stew. Sleeping was going to be an interrupted adventure by carefully scrutinizing every sound outside my room and similar to a James Bond movie, every set of footsteps that shuffled past my door had me imagining that "Odd Job", Bond's assistant, was going to come springing into my room in some sort of Kung Fu attack mode. I recall a few years ago, I was having breakfast at Bob Evans with a fellow manager friend of mine from another company in northeast Ohio. He told me that on his first business trip to China, he was so scared that he slept on the floor with his feet propped up against the door to protect against any break-ins. That seemed very odd in-between bites of eggs and sausage; now, fast forward two years and that wasn't funny to me at all; I actually considered it. This was the first time in my life I felt as though I were an outsider; I am now a stranger in a strange land and my fear factor was registering pretty high. At about this time, I flashbacked to my very first day at my company in March of 1974; I was getting $1.95 per hour to remove burrs from machined parts on a pedestal grinder with a wire brush. Does that really seem 30 years ago? No it doesn't and now I am leading a team to help my company secure a manufacturing foothold in China. You know, that de-burring job is sounding better each passing second. Anyway, I placed my head on the pillow, staring at the plain white ceiling and telling myself that God will protect me tonight; he has helped me through much harder situations, and this too shall pass. It seemed I was awake every other minute, but I did eventually fall into a sound sleep. Morning came and I met my fellow travelers in the hotel lobby to begin meeting suppliers. I dared not say a word about my fretful night of slumber and simply smiled and said, "I slept better than I thought," lying through each sip of coffee. We headed to visit our suppliers at their manufacturing plant and the city looked frightening; it was crowded beyond belief; it was messy, chaotic, dirty and pretty much like a third world city that I had imagined in my limited reading. When I saw the worker's dorms, a sick feeling hit me in the stomach; to quote Dorothy in the Wizard of Oz, "Toto, we are not in Kansas anymore." This surely was not Ohio where I live and it really became realistic at this point; I was half way around the world from my home. The urge to escape hit its zenith just as we pulled into the manufacturing plant's parking lot and then a revelation happened that I did not imagine.

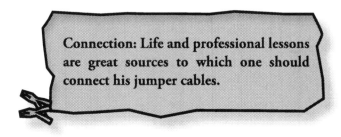

Connection: Life and professional lessons are great sources to which one should connect his jumper cables.

"Too many people are thinking of security instead of opportunity."
—James Byrnes

I am not really sure what I expected when I entered the factory doorway of the manufacturing plant, but what I saw was an absolutely spotless plant. The heat and humidity at the plant was what I experienced in Tallahassee, Florida in August, but not one worker flinched or complained; each diligently worked on his machine, totally ignoring the prevalent conditions. Sweat was pouring off my forehead but it probably would not have looked too professional if I complained considering the surrounding conditions. Every person I met in the plant showed me great kindness, respect, friendliness and a genuine feeling that I was royalty. Royalty from West Virginia born and raised Tim Dodd? I was genuinely touched by this reception and never envisioned it occurring. In fact, I was almost embarrassed by this outpouring to me from complete foreigners. The plant was abuzz in perfect synchronicity; the job orders flowed properly, the workers and machines seemed to be in syncopated rhythm, and the only sound on the shop floor was mechanical harmony. I was very, very impressed. I was witnessing manufacturing excellence and found this very exciting—no text book, power point, or operations review could describe what I was watching in person. **This was how production was meant to be.** The more I watched this, the more I began to realize how lucky I was to witness this world-class manufacturing excellence. If I could absorb this, ask some questions, and see the opportunities for improvement, my business knowledge would be at a much higher level and would certainly help me as a business leader at my company. I began to realize how comfortable I had become in my own manufacturing environment. I didn't realize it then, but this initial trip set the foundation for the success of my project in my fourth and fifth trips to this fascinating environment. Sometimes in life, attitude can be so negative and misery-based when faced with a new challenge that it looks far from appealing. But once one dips his toe into the water, the current can be inviting. I was picked to lead this project for one important reason; they knew I would get it done right. With my confidence, leadership, intelligence and gut feel of things, I would sail this ship with prevailing winds. As I walked around the plant, I began to feel like a lottery pick on National Basketball Association (NBA) draft night and every worker I met welcomed me the way the NBA commissioner does when one's name is called. Yes, my company made the right draft choice, and the "cables" were working; it just took me a while to see it. Now became the opportunity to really challenge myself to diligently, and productively, put everything I have learned into action.

"You can't tell someone to go out and lead. You become a leader by doing. So if you want to be a leader, go do it."
—Chuck Noll

Key Chapter Points:

1: *Change happens in life! We often can't control that, but we can adapt.*

2: *Fear can be paralyzing—it can also be a great source of motivation.*

3: *Sometimes in life, a situation we dread or have no interest in turns out to be a wonderful opportunity and growth experience.*

4: *Don't become comfortable! Look for ways to challenge yourself.*

CHAPTER 2

"Home, where my love lies waiting silently for me."

—Paul Simon

On my first flight back home from China, I was totally exhausted. Excluding some nice, group dinners, this trip was one hundred percent business; I had to have my "A Game" working the whole time and that is fatigue inducing, so there was no time for any Kodak moments on tour guided buses as some might expect. As I nestled in my Continental Airlines seat, the combination of long work hours, the time change, my own stress induced emotions, absence from my wife, shoulder-to-shoulder with my peers all day and night, and adapting to a foreign country and a new employment experience all caught up with me. I took a few deep breaths, rubbed my eyes and reflected on my inaugural week in China. It was too much in too little time to mentally digest and I will admit I was still pressing the "I am Irked" button repeatedly for being selected to lead this project. Prior to this appointment, my director position was a well earned role and I had it unceremoniously yanked from my grasp and replaced with an overseas project manager role with the intent for a developmental opportunity.

> *I have learned that offering no forgiveness only adds up to bitterness and no relief from my own anger or disappointment.*

It was still causing me some heartburn as the jumbo jet lifted off, but there is a reason forgiveness is peppered throughout the Bible; it is hard to practice, but very important to implement and will just take some time. It also dawned on me about this time that several more China trips were in my crystal ball, with the next one being only three weeks out. Most people may not run the same errand to Walgreen's to pick up a prescription every three weeks and I was going to be transported across the globe again in less than a month. I am slowly learning to deal with one headache at a time. I am eager to get back home to America, see my wife, talk to my girls, dress informally, and sleep in my own bed. If one wants to really appreciate the greatness of our country and it's freedoms, leave "Old GLORY" and one will be glad to be under its shelter.

One benefit of long business trips is that one is usually forced to think and reflect. One can kill some time watching a movie, reading a book, or trying to sleep, but there will be long chunks of time looking out the plane's oval window into a wilderness of cloudy nothingness and now have your own thoughts to invade one's thinking. It was about five hours or so into this flight that I began to have one of these see-through window times that I really began to think about leadership and what it means to me. My company valued me as a leader and I did not take that lightly. I was receiving a nice monthly paycheck to lead a team which would help the company achieve financial profitability. I must say, I think I felt successful, but what exactly defines a good leader? I had been to several leadership classes and have always profited minimally from books. I have read the words and picked up usable bits of information, but the underlying question still remained, "What makes **Me** a good leader?" Where do I verbally lead others? Do I lead them to my thoughts and wishes? Do I lead them to look within their own hearts and find their desires and passions? Do I show them by actions and words to see a bigger picture? The hardest and most personal question of all is introspection: **Would I want to work for me?** Good leaders are not only hard to find but also harder to develop. One can easily lose the "good manager" moniker and be relegated to being an "incompetent manager." There was no way in my lifetime that the title "incompetent manager" was going to be applied to my name. This train of thought led me thinking about National Football League (NFL) coaches; I have always been a football fan and I was pondering what made some NFL coaches great and others forgotten. This profession has its leadership prowess placed under the magnifying glass almost every day during the NFL season and the more I thought about the great coaches, the more interesting my thoughts became. These greats automatically entered my mind and I analyzed what made them great?

Coach	Leadership Trait
Bud Grant	Stone faced, no emotion, authoritative
John Madden	Crazily energized, animated, hyper
Tom Landry	Poised, professional, innovative, in control
Bill Walsh	Intelligent, calm, almost professor-like
Chuck Noll	Blue collar style, firm, rough edged

Five great leaders, all in the Football Hall of Fame. Forever winners. In my opinion, all belong on the Mount Rushmore of great coaches.

How complete is your definition of leadership and success?

Where am I; where are you as we look at these coaching styles? Each one has a different list of leadership traits and in each one of these coaches I have delicately picked certain attributes, but am not totally aligned with any one. I became a Bud Grant sitting in my bosses' office when revolutionizing a 60 year method of manufacturing machined parts. To get a team motivated, I have been a John Madden in an off site meeting, almost embarrassing each member when a business plan I was working on did not properly pan out. When I was Tom Landry, I had to address a sensitive human resources issue with a machine operator. I thoughtfully admired Bill Walsh when I mentored a young individual contributor to becoming a supervisor. I tried to equal Chuck Noll when I introduced new ideas and processes to the shop floor associates that they would be required to follow and understand. The point here is that Leadership is not a "one recipe fits all" casserole; it is more of a hodge-podge of ingredients that when properly combined lead to leadership excellence. I try to work on this daily; I have my wife's support; I use my educational and work experience; I practice my faith to make sound decisions (that can often effect the lives of many people and for the China project, a whole direction for my company) and a gut feeling formed by the combination. I feel neither shame nor bravado calling myself a leader.

Connection: What is the source that you will connect your Jumper Cables to in order to overcome the initial obstacles encountered early in your journey?

Once I came to this conclusion, I found myself very sleepy so I took a restful nap and an hour or so later the plane was touching down at Cleveland Hopkins Airport in Ohio, USA, after a brief stop at Chicago's O'Hare airport. It was late at night and the airport was practically uninhabited. Only a few maintenance men are moving about, shops are closed and the place looks coma-like. As the moving sidewalk takes me to the main terminal, I think about what I have seen the past eight days: the people, the customs, the towns, the gracious hospitality bestowed upon me, one amazing production facility and a new stamp in my passport. I get to the parking deck, slide into the front seat of my car, pay the parking fee and head south on the Ohio highway. Lynyrd Skynyrd's "Sweet Home Alabama" comes on the radio and I smile and tap the steering wheel in unison to the song. The only leadership I want right now is for my car to lead me to home. "Big wheels keep on turning, carry me home to my kin"; As the speedometer reaches 75 m.p.h., it occurs to me that I have heard this song 500 times but it has never sounded as meaningful as tonight.

Key Chapter Points:

1:    No one trait makes a great leader.

2:    Leadership style is comprised of segments from inspirational sources.

3:    Identify what is the driving force behind abilities to lead.

4:    Ask the hard questions—where is my current direction heading?

5:    Reflection—think about the whole, big picture, not just the pieces.

CHAPTER 3

"In that direction," the cat said, waving its right paw round, "lives a Hatter: and in that direction," waving the other paw, "lives a March Hare. Visit either you like: they're both mad."
"But I don't want go among mad people," Alice remarked.
"Oh, you can't help that," said the Cat: "we're all mad here. I'm mad. You're mad."
"How do you know I'm mad?" said Alice.
"You must be," said the Cat, "or you wouldn't have come here."

—"Alice in Wonderland"

In the movie, "Born on the 4th of July," one of the most disturbing scenes was when Ron Kovic (the paralyzed soldier who is the protagonist of the film) returns home from the Vietnam War, wheelchair bound. He is in a local town parade and instead of being hailed upon by well wishers and civilians as America's townspeople did for those soldiers returning home from World Wars I and II, he is met with obscene gestures, rude comments, and anger from the neighbors as he wheels himself in the parade. One lesson learned from that scene is how many times we anticipate and expect a sunny reception for an act or job we do, but instead are met with the total opposite—a coldness that can only be explained by experience and the heart ache that follows. The Monday morning I returned to work after my first overseas excursion to China, was certainly unexpectedly bizarre, peculiar, and unusual. I have always had a the knack of identifying the mood and temperament of those around me—family, co-workers, friends, church goers, etc. Many times I have been in a business staff meeting and before the first word is uttered, I can tell right away what the mood will be for the next hour. When I settled in at work that morning, it did not take long for me to sense a high degree of resentment and betrayal towards me (especially among the hourly associates). Instead of getting a pat-on-the back and appreciative accolades for getting the China Project moving forward, I was picking up an unfamiliar frosty vibe from those who had once worked with me. I was (NOT BY CHOICE) the lucky lottery winner to lead this lengthy China project and I was getting greeted by ice men and women. The reason for these ill feelings was the "perception" that I was moving our Ohio-based jobs to China. I was being viewed as the on that was igniting this fire sale of Ohio jobs. I thought, "Are we all Mad"? Now, lets get something totally straight and without a shred of miscommunication: I bleed corporate blue; out of thousands or so associates in my company in the United States, only about 30 or so have more seniority than I do in terms of length of service to the company. With my 40th anniversary with my company several years away, it is extremely safe to say that I have given this company its money's worth! Now take that sentence and complement it with my fervent stance on not wanting to expand the company's brand into China. You can now visualize how this negative reception I received hurt to the core. In fact, this mood that was circulating and building during my absence was one of the worst atmospheres I have had to endure while working at my company. It almost had me feeling as though I was being mentored by Lebron James, a basketball talent unmatched, when in actuality, nothing could be further from the truth. I was not mimicking him by "taking my talents to South Beach" (or more perceived "taking my company's talents to the far East"). Again, it was 'perception" that was triggering this sentiment and in so many occurrences in life, we use perception instead of factual intervention to reach our conclusions. I have done it too many times and it has back fired at me. I had been with my company for three decades in North East Ohio and I was doing all I could to keep building the illustrious company's name and maintaining our profitability while staying firmly in place here. It was a "tap on the shoulder" that led me to China and not raising my hand as Arnold Horshack did in the ol' "Welcome Back Kotter" days to be selected. This project was only beginning to make me feel as though I had become an island to my cohorts; this feeling of betrayal in the air only exacerbated this isolationist persona. I could almost detect my associates huddling in the lunch room talking about China rumors and how we were all going to lose our jobs as many manufacturing companies unfortunately have had to experience in the mid west. Though not using these words, the associates were probably mentally echoing the meaning of Admiral Perry's' famous quip, "We have met the enemy and they are ours" as they shot menacing glances towards my office. Innocently, I have inherited a project I did not want and now my co-workers are deciding to blame me for this. This is a bad dream becoming unbearable. Can it get worse? Is my annual colonoscopy coming up? Is the IRS calling on line two?

"Some clubs want to win so much they'll do anything to get it. Our approach has been just the opposite. We've tried to do things the right way. And the right way is the rules and regulations and they are precisely what we go by. I may not like all of them, but once they are in, we play by them."
—Don Shula

By this point, it was time to stop the "woe is me" attitude and get on with the task laid down before me. This China project was not going to be completed in a two-hour-lock-my-office-door-and-leave-me-alone time frame; it was going to take weeks and months (by the way, for those of you keeping track at home, my China trip box score totaled 12 visits in 22 months. Think about that the next time your flight to Disney is running 30 minutes behind schedule)! My "Mad Hatter" was no longer directing the Company's General Industry Service Group, but instead was having international conference calls on a daily basis, staying up to 11 pm so the phone meetings I direly needed were on the Chinese time zone work schedule. Next calling our General Manager and Human Resources Manager who would then redirect my messages to city commissioners, planning and zoning personnel, construction outfits, utility companies, and those in the loop. We are all Mad! Remember I am dealing with a foreign country that is not English speaking, so relying on my interpreter and others to guide me was essential but also left a doubt of fear at times if my message was quoted correctly. This was a whole new experience for me and it was self revealing; it taught me much about my confidence in my own abilities; it gave me a stronger sense of business acumen and urgency, dealing with foreign relations, and international networking. Reflecting on this project was the greatest three years in my professional life. The contagious leper project that I initially wanted absolutely no part of actually turned out to be the greatest memory of my time at my company. The whole experience impacted who I am today. How is that possible? I am still one of the hardest people to get my decisions to sway. Once I decide an answer, a resolution, or a solution; my adversaries better have an arsenal of facts, case studies, and money saving information to get me to change my point of view. So if I would have been told in June of 2004 that this project was going to be the line item on my future plan of which I would have been the most proud, I would have bet my house against that being true. If it were true my wife and I would now be living in a tent along the road. There is a very transparent object lesson to be learned here. Human nature tends to lean towards "change is bad" when something new is thrown at us. Sometimes in a rather unmitigated fashion we tend to internally stomp our feet and scream similar to Herman Muenster, "No, No, No, No" when a new proposition is laid before us. But if we take a step back and analyze the goal and start planning a reference line to attain that goal and incorporate what we will need to reach that destination (tools, experiences, resources, funds, etc.), then the worrisome "How do I begin?" this project starts to materialize. That initial first step (though it may be small at first) can be the hardest domino to push over, but can start a chain reaction that will lead to the desired outcome. The more entwined I became in the China Project, the more the initial entanglements began to unwind. Progress was beginning to happen and that was both exciting and satisfying. Plans were starting to take shape in a more defined pattern; communications were not as strained, and energy was building, I was much more engaged, and my fear that was an initial hindrance was turning into a metamorphosis of getting things done and getting them done the right way on time. One of the members of my leadership team enjoys running marathons and he once told me that when everything is clicking well in the race, one doesn't fear the part of the race when the wall is hit and every step becomes painful; one now becomes so focused that he or she knows when the next mile marker is going to pop up without even looking up. It does not happen every race, but when it does, one better believe that this race is going to fall into the "better" category instead of the "let's forget this one" column. Once I got the negative "I can't" and "why me?" feelings out of my head, I began to see the fruits of my labor slowly ripening instead of wilting, I was replacing these depressing words with promise, hope, and visualization of a desired outcome. I was seeing the mile markers of my progress clip on by without any slowing down. There was not going to be the dreaded wall that marathoners fear. I was not going to allow it. The fruits of my labor will pay off.

Connection: Realize that the difficult situations are temporary and offer opportunities to learn—both professionally and personally.

So what was the magic trick I pulled from the hat to allow me to come to this realization? Attitude is the magic abstract noun. I changed it to allow me to focus my energies on determination, progress, action, and self change for the betterment of those who have placed their trust in me. Again, I was somewhat blind to this in the embryonic stages, but as the project began to build muscle, it was very apparent. Funny how we throw around the statements, "Change your attitude . . . . I don't like your attitude . . . . Your attitude is terrible . . . . His attitude is so negative . . . . She copped a real attitude . . . ." Almost universally, words that are associated with attitude tend be downers, when people are able to change their attitude for the betterment, there might not be a better self—improvement they can bestow upon themselves. When I select a team at work, do I always look for the best, the smartest or the most business savvy? Not at all. What I do look for is the right attitude that will be brought to the team. The ones who believe in teamwork, can do, let's roll up our sleeves and get something done, and when faced with adversary, will perform best. Think back to the 1980 US Olympic Hockey team. So much has been written and discussed about that team, but in comparison to the Russian team (which without question was the world's best at that time). The US team was less experienced, less used to playing in high pressure games, much younger, and in all honesty, less talented. How did they win? Great leadership and game plan by Coach Herb Brooks, who had a great desire and we will not lose attitude. If these two teams played 100 times, the Soviet team would have probably won 90 times, but not on the night when it mattered most. A positive, upbeat attitude may simply be the greatest tool we have for success and once I got my attitude right sized, I knew my project was going to work out without a doubt. Absolutely no doubt.

"We all came together six months before the 1980 Winter Olympics with different styles of hockey and different ethnic beliefs . . . but we made ourselves a team. Individually, we could not have done it."
—Mike Eruzione, Captain, US 1980 Hockey Team

Key Chapter Points:

1: Better understand the business decisions that don't align with your opinions—you can still adhere to your values, but the company's directives must be followed.

2: Initial perceptions are not always factual and accurate.

3: Visualize progress, overcoming obstacles and look for the progress.

CHAPTER 4

"Doing anything well doesn't just lead to success—it is success. Real success in life begins with acceptance—acceptance of God's belief in you as a unique and special person."

—Kyle Rote Jr.

I have always liked the cliché, "jump start the motivation department." It is unique, because even though one can replace other words in this cliché for motivation such as inspiration, determination, quality, maturity, self awareness, etc., employees are not working up to their potential, it is a temptation to want to use a proverbial swift kick in their motivational derriere to jump start the potential career/ project/education/ or in some instances to just plain grow up! It has been said by more than one male co-worker of mine that the kick is one attribute of mine which I have perfected. I am not totally sure when I acquired this talent; was it watching my father who had a minor disability? A wonderful man, but his disability sometimes became a crutch. He often refused to take risks or face challenges presented to him. This caused my dad much frustration. As

I grew up, it caused me frustration in watching his disability get the upper hand on my father. To quote the musical group "The Eagles," "So often times it happens that we live our lives in chains, and we never even know we have the key." That was my father and I think part of my motivation to be great and see others in the same light comes from him. Another lovely person who helped me achieve high levels of motivation was my sister, Becky. In the winter of 1975, she lost a courageous battle with leukemia. To this day, losing her makes little sense to my earthly thinking and, though it is true that time heals wounds, the pain is always with me. The degree of 'hurt' varies, but the pain never leaves. For whatever reason, when people die many years before 'their time' rationality fails to make sense, seems unfair and thus not comforting. it just is not fair. I think about Becky and her fire to live when she was facing an awful disease helps me stay motivated; she will always be living inside my heart. My mother is another source for my motivational stride. She can be very kind, but imbedded in her DNA make up are traits such as, selfishness, always having the spot light directed on her, comfortably placing herself in the victim role, and requiring a lot of maintenance. Mom also has an unforgiving stubbornness that I often have to battle with on a near daily basis as her primary guardian and decision maker; it is not an enviable task at all and often leads to frustration and resentment on my behalf. But you know what? That stubbornness that dear old mama embraces is pretty well instilled in me and I think has helped to make me a strong leader. If you think about it, tell me a great leader that was not stubborn? Whether it is a military leader, top shelf coach, captain of industry, or idolized politician, the genetic trait of stubbornness is pretty well imbedded in their DNA and helps make the tough decisions. Stubbornness is also very motivating—"I am doing this way BECAUSE!! And no one is going to change my mind!!" My lovely wife, my wife, may be the number one person that has supplied me motivation—a blind date led us to courtship and our marriage in 1975 and my wife was the 'kick in my motivation department" to convince me to go back to college and get not one, not two, but **three** degrees. It was a hard juggling act to work full time, be a devoted family man and go to college at night for my Associate's, Bachelor's and Master's in Engineering, Management, and Business. But with unyielding support from my wife and a dedicated timeline to make it happen, I earned those degrees that helped catapult me to higher levels of managerial responsibility in my company. That **NEVER** would have occurred without my higher education and my wife was the catalyst to make it happen. Again, my wife has been number one on my personal Billboard chart for many years and my motivation to succeed is deeply indebted to her always being there for me. My two daughters are very different but also similar in many ways—they are very caring for those less fortunate, devoted to their family, and very driven and successful women—it is interesting, when they were small girls, we always stressed to them the importance of finding what you want in life and going for it like a runway train—both my wife and I taught them compassion, kindness, taking nothing for granted and being appreciative for each waking day. And as they are both grown ladies now, I see that the fruits of our parenting have blossomed beautifully and it is often our daughters showing and telling my wife and myself the same lessons of life we first taught them in the early 1980's! "What comes around, goes around," and I could not be happier or prouder of my little girls. Watching them grow up and succeed in life is truly motivating for me to get out of bed each morning face whatever challenges life decides to toss my way. Also, having a two grand daughters has allowed me to enter the grand parent phase of my life with even more appreciation than I did as a parent. Boy, talk about having someone wrapped around their tiny, tiny finger! I would be remiss if I did not mention my personal relationship with God as being very motivational for me to live each day—I do not know how else to say it, but the Lord has been gracious beyond words to me—he has granted me a loving family, a very stable job that has allowed us to live comfortably and have many luxuries in life, he has given me strength to be a healthy man and has provided me wisdom to make difficult decisions when faced with them. Becky's favorite biblical verse was "I can do everything through Christ who gives me strength." I completely agree and owe everything I have achieved to God—it is my faith in God that is the motivational fuel I need to carry on each day regardless of what new battles we are facing.

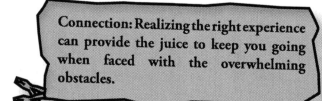

Connection: Realizing the right experience can provide the juice to keep you going when faced with the overwhelming obstacles.

I think I can say without reservation that the people mentioned in this chapter are the motivational flames that have kept my fire for life burning brightly—as a father, son, brother, husband, grand father, friend, neighbor, church parishioner, and manager and associate of my great company. Sure, over the years, I have had snippets of motivation come from various sources: authors, church leaders, coaches, co-workers, friends, etc., but my starting line up will always be my family with the Lord as my pilot. Now, this all being put in print, I have realized that the motivational gift I have does not bode well to those I come in contact with that give me excuses or reasons for not working up to their hundred percent potential or lackluster effort. I expect team work, full effort and fulfillment from all those that work for me—do you want to see me place my ceremonial shoe in someone's rear end when I sense their motivation is dwindling? Have them tell me:

"I can't get my college degree because I do not have the time."

"We can't change this process—it has always been done this way."

"He is just an hourly worker—we can easily replace him."

"I would like to make a change with (fill in the blank), but I am scared of the outcome."

It is statements like these that make my managerial blood boil—these are all excuses and excuses don't create anything except more excuses! When I am encountered with one of these face to face situation's, don't expect me to be portraying Father Murphy providing guidance and insight. I am going to want answers and you better be prepared to give them to me. To quote legendary great football coach, Lou Holtz, "Don't tell me how rocky the sea is, just bring the darn ship in." I expect that from myself and expect that from those around me. Nothing great was ever accomplished by laying down a lame excuse. Nothing . . .

"Failures are expected by losers, ignored by winners."
—Joe Gibbs

Key Chapter Points:

1: Identify the sources of your motivation.

2: Identify how that motivational source is initiated and sustained.

3: Excuses never satisfy—they simply stall progress.

4: Identify your support team and cheerleaders.

CHAPTER 5

"I am proud of all my trophies, but truthfully when I was playing, I never thought of my records. I just tried to do all I possibly could to help the team win."

—Roy Campanella

In the 1995 Oscar Award winning film, "Apollo 13," starring Tom Hanks, there is a remarkable scene when mission control in Houston, Texas, realizes that the Apollo spaceship is facing severe uncertainty when attempting to re-enter the earth's atmosphere. The team assembled in Houston has a lively debate on what it needs do to bring the astronauts back to planet earth without dire consequences. The team comes up with an energy conservation plan as well as a detailed sequence of contacting every engineer, technician, and production worker who helped assemble the spacecraft. The conclusion was very simple: **"failure was not an option"** and was spoken with authority by the leader of the control team and every team member went into high gear to assure that the astronauts returned home safely. The astronauts all made it back to earth without incident and actually this clause was never really stated during the Apollo's mission; it made for a terrific scene for the movie and was very memorable; it was also a foreshadowing for a future project I helped to lead.

In 2011, one of the production facilities I was overseeing was facing an interesting predicament. For over 60 years, the machines in this plant would take 12 foot bars of stainless steel and have them precision cut to make components to be used as the building blocks for assembly into other products that another leg of our facility produced. This process had worked very well for decades and I don't think anyone thought it needed any tweaking. Colloquially speaking, "If it ain't broke, don't mess with it." But with demand for our products exponentially increasing and constraints being placed on me as a manager neither to hire more people, nor to out-source the work plus space limitations for more machines, I had to think of new methods to improve productivity under these controlling conditions. Each passing day was placing me slightly deeper in the productivity hole, so I had to devise a way (or ways) the team could improve the efficiency of this process. Simply put, when the machines were in operation, they would cut a segment of the 12 foot bar stock and this would drop a perfectly machined component; though working well, it was not enough production to keep up with our ever rising demand. I assembled our engineering team and posed the following question, "How can we produce more parts?" This question has probably been said and re-said and re-re-said in production meetings all over the globe, but it needed to be addressed. I received some normal responses:

"We are currently running through the breaks and lunches."

"We have done a different shifting strategy of 24 hours per day, seven days a week."

"We really have exhausted all ways to make the machines more productive."

These answers had more than a kernel of merit, but were not going to suffice; we needed more output. At this point, I suggested the following proposition, "How do we make two parts at a time instead of one?" At first, you would have thought there was a deer in the headlights as the team went silent with stares and nervous shuffling of pens and papers.

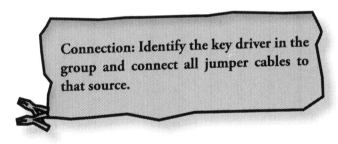

Connection: Identify the key driver in the group and connect all jumper cables to that source.

But once this query began to start processing in the minds of my engineers, the "a-ha" moment took over. One team member thought that with a few minimal adjustments, his machine could possibly drop two parts simultaneously; he then began to explain how this might be possible. Soon, he became the inspiration to become introspective. I challenged each team member to emulate the one who spoke up and put all collective thoughts together and see what develops. We dubbed this project "Apollo 13" with the tag line, "Failure is not an option." Obviously, our machining project did not have the urgency of the Houston mission control team, but I wanted our team to know that, unlike some engineering or research and development projects which can drag on for what seems like *ad infinitum*, I was receiving pressure from upper management and I wanted to place a fire under the collective rear ends of this team. Small successes came rather quickly. The team's ideas and collaboration proved fruitful; energy was building; enthusiasm was growing, and there was a harmonious buzz in the plant as word circulating about this new process. The initial skeptics who said "this can't be done," were being outnumbered by team members who were making it happen! Even though long hours became the norm for this project (including many weekends and evening hours), there was a definite positive atmosphere and everyone chipped in to make this project be a success. As a manager, I was thoroughly impressed and proud of what I was witnessing. In only 30 days, the team was able to begin producing two parts on two different machines with the strict cycle and quality parameters that the company demanded. Think about this: **in one month**, this team was able to double the output on a procedure that had been standard work for **720 months!** This is a classic example for definition of process optimization. For countless years, we were told that the machines were red lining and running at maximum output. It just goes to prove the fact that when a team is assembled with the right guidance, motivation, and direction, a change can be made that in many cases will eventually become the standard for future usage. I recently read an article about the evolution of the Indianapolis 500 motor cars. In 1939, a rear engine car was first used and was scoffed at by traditionalists, but in 1965, a rear engine car took the checkered flag. The thinking behind the rear engine car was that by having the motor behind the driver, the car's balance would be better distributed and cornering could be more efficient and prevent less wear on the car. Four years later, **every** car in the Indy line up was motored by a rear engine. That is what often happens when change is presented in manufacturing—the first-thought-in-one's-head-attitude is one of "NO," but when it is actually analyzed, case studied, small batch sampled, and finally uploaded to full scale production and shown to work, the "nay-sayers" quickly want to jump on the bandwagon of "being with the team all along!" Once the obstacles and adversity for "Apollo 13" morphed into "determination-for-our destination," the momentum began to snow ball and the end result was not only a double drop being introduced, but also the confidence and success began to spread to other parts of the plant. All employees were standing a bit taller and with their chests puffed out (and rightfully so!), and were taking greater ownership of their accomplishments. It was a super rippling effect to see unfolding. A great take-a-way that came from this was associates looking at other parts of their daily work and seeing how they could improve efficiencies; how they could reduce waste; how they could find ways to save money for the plant? From a business perspective, this project was screaming "WIN". A reduction in labor hours resulted along with more capacity in the plant. From an associate's perspective, it showed that the voice of innovation and process optimization was encouraged and not squelched (as is often the case in traditional manufacturing settings). It allowed more risk taking to take center stage and not be afraid of one's ideas but be confident and share them. Though they may not always be possible, in the right cases, this confidence can lead to ideas that can become realities. Plus, as mentioned earlier, it was a time for the associates to smile and take pride in a new system; it was a new way of doing things; it was a change for the good of all concerned. Once operating at high efficiency, I was able to have several members of my company's executive team including the president of the organization, walk through our plant to see this new process in full scale operation. Usually when the president of a company walks through the plant floor, nerves will be on red alert, tensions will be high, the fear of saying the wrong thing will be ever present and everyone will be metaphorically walking on eggshells. But when our president walked through and saw this new procedure unfold in front of him, he was very impressed and appreciative to see manufacturing innovation taking place. In fact, he even grabbed a pair of safety goggles, rolled up his sleeves and actually got into the operations of the machine to better understand the new ingenuity right in front of his eyes (yes, I was a just a tad nervous at this point to be sure the "double drop" worked as advertised, but it did with a quiet "pheeeeew" coming from my exhalation). I could not be prouder. As a manager this was one of those great leadership moments for me because the team was coming together and clicking on all cylinders. Success was breeding, and the process change that had been exhorted as "no way" was now reality; it was if the whole team was wearing a success laden headdress with rows of colorful feathers. What ever happens in my future with the company is always unknown , but I know that when my time to leave finally arrives, being part of the "Apollo 13" project is one that I will always cherish and for which I will always be proud.

**"There are thousands to tell you it cannot be done,
There are thousands to prophesy failure;
There are thousands to point out to you one by one,**

The dangers that wait to assail you.
But just buckle it in with a bit of a grin,
Just take off your coat and go to it;
Just start to sing as you tackle the thing
That "couldn't be done," and you'll do it."
-Edgar Guest

Key Chapter Points:

1: *Keep asking 'How' and 'Why' questions.*

2: *The synergy of a team working towards a goal is vital for success.*

3: *Don't fear 'out of the box' thinking; cherish it! Give change a chance.*

4: *Celebratetheteam'saccomplisments—Success breeds Success!*

5: *Remove the word 'failure' from your vocabulary.*

CHAPTER 6

"People acting together as a group can accomplish things which no individual acting alone could ever hope to bring about."

—Franklin D. Roosevelt

Think how nerve racking and tense it is to build a new house. One is dealing with architects, review boards, zoning regulations, contractors, suppliers, electricians, plumbers, etc. Hopefully, one is living nearby while planning that new home. Now put this new home building concept on an exponential dosage of steroids and try to visualize and imagine building a new factory in a completely foreign country where one doesn't speak the language, is a neophyte to the culture, and is heavily relying on input from others about neighborhoods, local laws, viable locations, and all the intangibles. It can be quite intimidating. And just for the clichéd icing on the cake, the job and professional reputation is riding on this icing being the most palatable finishing touch. This makes for a prolonged Maalox moment to say the least!

This apprehension was present the first few trips I made to China, but by about the fourth journey I noticed the initial hurdles were appearing to be lower in height and I was able to make more successful bounds over them without trip-ups. By this time, we had narrowed our search for our new production facility to four locations (or zones as the Chinese refer to them). This was an intensely hectic time with many obstacles reaching out their sticky tentacles. To alleviate these obstructions, I was holding more and more detailed question and answer sessions, increasing my meetings with local officials, being sure to get a handle on the number of resources we were going to need for our factory to be firmly installed, {such as water supplies and electricity (including back ups)}, and maybe most importantly of all, finding and training a skilled labor pool. As I had done on each trip to China, I made it a point to seek out two to three manufacturing/processing/warehousing/distribution facilities which had an English speaking general manager to gather as much information as I could about the locales we were pondering, the pool of candidates we were considering, and listening for any other "inside scoop". These meetings were memorable for me in many ways: they provided information, helped establish business relationships (which are so vital for success in the Chinese culture) provided a coincidental Disneyesque—case of "It's a Small World After all". One of the mayors I met in a local province had a college-age daughter who was attending the University of Illinois at the same time, my oldest daughter was living in Champaign, Illinois, working at a local bank. The mayor suggested my daughter give his daughter some financial counseling on her spending habits! It was a light hearted moment which helped to solidify our relationship, build trust, bench mark, and bridge the western way of doing business with the host-eastern method. The results were tremendous. One idea that came from these exchanges was to visit local trade schools in the various regions (it was like going back in time). It was absolutely essential that for our plant to be successful we needed a strong pipeline of qualified workers wherever we decided to break ground. After more meetings and reciprocal conversations, we decided on my team's recommendation that a province two hours from Shanghai, China would be the home of our manufacturing facility. It was a superb location in a trade-free zone, with a community feeding a local school nearby providing the life blood to the plant—a trained stream of labor. It was close to a port to allow for import/export considerations. We negotiated a very fair lease price for the land and an hour away from the plant we had our equipment supplier providing training. The water, electricity and other resources were also plentiful and easy to access as well. The final touch was that this region was able to provide us with a temporary factory until our new one was completely constructed in about one year. This was an immense milestone for me in my professional career; we had thoroughly done our homework and were confident with our recommendation to our executive team.

Connection: With the jumper cables connected and successes being realized, remember the important matter is the successes on the journey are milestones; important lessons to be captured and practiced.

Once I had the bulkhead of the China Project completed, it allowed me to reflect on this very enjoyable chapter of my professional career. However, in a strange business intertwined irony, my successes liquefied into obstacles when the project was handed off to the new manager in China. When the project was completed, I lost my director title (which took years to acquire) and I was assigned to integrate a new acquisition in Ohio. This hand-off was not fumbled, but as I carried the ball, my apathy barometer was rising and my focus on a goal was drastically dwindling. I saw this new phase of my managerial career as a demotion and it made me realize I had reached the pinnacle of my career and this was the denouement. I would not be going any higher with this company—lateral moves were more in line; climbing up the proverbial corporate ladder was no longer going to be a newsy item. The focus was turning toward younger talent within the organization. This realization caused considerable introspection on my behalf; it made me pay attention to the fact that success is not based on who you are, but you still are that person you see when looking into the mirror. A prime example is a list of outstanding National League Football Hall of Fame quarterbacks:

Dan Fouts	Dan Marino	Sonny Jurgensen
Jim Kelly	Warren Moon	Fran Tarkenton

All six have one noticeable thing in common: <u>they never won a Super Bowl</u>. Many appearances, but no golden ring. Does that fact make them any less successful? Does that fact tarnish their NFL careers? Are their enshrined busts in a different room in Canton, Ohio from other Super Bowl winning quarterbacks? Absolutely not. To me, success will always be a journey and not a destination. It is an on-going process that is constantly changing. On my resume, success should never appear as satisfying. It should be a stimulus to reach and attain higher goals, to produce faster, to strive longer, and never be content with the status quo. In my success portfolio, there must be strict adherence to quality with no cutting corners, and modeling honesty, fair play, high ethical standards, and respect for those involved. All my endeavors should be performed under the watchful scrutiny of the Lord's eye. I firmly believe that my model for success is to have unyielding determination towards my (or my team's) destination. My team and I will build the ladder on which we climb, paying very careful attention to the solid footing of each rung to help us reach the summit.

"Take a chance! All life is a chance. The man who goes farthest is generally the one who is willing to do and dare. The sure thing boat never gets far from shore."
-Andrew Carnegie

Key Chapter Points:

1: *Some of the greatest professional experience in life can occur when its not wanted.*

2: *Success is great to achieve, but it is never totally satisfying. Success should create motivation to drive for higher success.*

3: *Hard work, dedication and relationship building were all key components for success.*

CHAPTER 7

"Success is what you do with the ability that you have, how you use your talent. It doesn't necessarily mean any one thing. It could be any menial job. If you are the best or one of the best at that job, you have given everything of yourself and you know it. You have to live with yourself. That's Success!"

-George Allen

This is my Signature for Achievement:

Disability, Obstacle, Determination, Destination

Our culture tends to anecdotally state, "Let's start at the beginning" when one tells a saga or a new project arises. But in the quest for success, I discount that starting point and instead reverse the proceeding and start at the end. If you go back to my preface, the end is the final puzzle piece of my signature of achievement: the end is the destination. In order to have a destination, the following questions should be asked: Where Am I going? Why am I headed there? What are my motives and purposes and How will I know when I have arrived? Let's review my achievement signature in more detail.

Disability represents a challenge that may be a starting point towards the journey to success. What is the disability that is preventing you from beginning your journey? How can you use your disability for motivation? I think my father's hip-related disability placed self-imposed limitations on his progress and ultimately on his thriving for life. He gave in to the disability. It won. He didn't fight it. It was sad to witness . . . .

Obstacle can be the nemesis to success; I call it kryptonite. Obstacles may not always be visible, but are excuse barriers we erect to stop us from reaching our desired outcome. For me, my obstacles started at a young age; I was reared with little direction, no money, no true pedigree, and no real sense of bettering myself. I had a strike against me before I could even walk and strike two was coming down the pike. It was not the best of upbringings; it was an antithesis from a Norman Rockwell illustration of a happy suburban family. Any time one starts a sentence with, "I can't do this because . . . ." one has placed an obstacle in the field of view. Obstacles can be controlling; they can make one question a known entity versus an unknown one. They can be caused by a lack of support, a lack of money, a lack of education, a lack of health, and in the worst case of all, a lack of effort.

Determination may be called many things: grit, purpose, fortitude, passion, drive, desire, mission, fuel? Now take any or all of those and gift wrap it tightly in commitment and one has determination. Simply put, determination is whatever resolution one subscribes to in order to get to the destination and squelch any obstacles. Determination stands on four equally substantial legs that never, never, ever let one down.

Destination is one's goal; the victory, the pinnacle of the mountain. Whether it is the finish line, financial freedom, a dream home, a new job, a degree, weight loss, starting a new family, health, faith, driver's license or countless other end results; only you can define your achievement for yourself (especially if the destination is a very personal one). It is essential to always keep your destination in view. Whether that means taking baby steps at first when taking your first college class towards a doctorate degree or changing behavior to slim down. The destination must never leave you—it can be roaming around on the back roads of your daily thoughts, but must always be present. It may lead you to ask why you are going in a certain direction, but whatever pathway you choose, DODD will get you there. No short cuts, overcome all disabilities and obstacles, and determination will facilitate your reaching that destination.

Connection: See the destination first and begin to layout the path for the journey from where you are today.

I have two very different scenarios of achieving success. The first scenario involves my marathon buddy with whom I work. It took him six years and 12 attempts to finally qualify to run the Boston Marathon and another year and three more marathons to finally arrive in Boston. For those of you who do not know, Boston is the Mecca for marathons and outside of the Olympics; it is the only marathon in which one has to qualify to participate making it a select group. Seven years is a pretty long time however he had no disabilities, but faced plenty of obstacles: tough marathon courses, stringent time standards, and at times self-doubt. But he learned something from each race. He started training with a group all of whom had the same dream to qualify except he trained differently he tried race strategies and began to gain confidence at each experience. In 2006, he missed by 15 minutes and then by seven minutes; in 2007 he missed by two minutes, and in 2008 his "jumper cables" kicked in. He told me that as long as he stayed healthy, he was going to finally qualify; the question was only when? Every day, EVERY DAY for those seven years a Boston thought or two would pop into his head and he had the vision to make the Boston Marathon Dream become a reality. His destination happened in 2010. It became real when he completed the race and the finisher's medal was placed around his neck. "Dream your painting, then paint your dream" is his favorite quote and it works for me.

The 2nd scenario was in the 1999 National College Athletic Association (NCAA) men's basketball tournament. The final game came down to the University of Connecticut vs. Duke. All season, Duke was the best team and it showed in the tournament as they played exceedingly well. UCONN had to work harder and the championship game was a classic nail biter with UCONN coming out the victor by three points. After the game in the press conference, UCONN's head coach, Jim Calhoun, was asked how his team prepared for Duke in such a short time. He told the reporters that the end of every practice all season, his team would focus on a few plays and tactics to try to beat Duke. Think about that—these two teams are not in the same conference and would only play each other in the NCAA tournament, but Coach Calhoun was preparing his team all season long to play the best team. He knew that if his team kept winning, he would eventually have a battle with Duke and when it mattered most, his Huskies rose to the challenge to beat the Blue Devils in a very memorable game. For Coach Calhoun, winning the tournament was the destination: overcoming losses, player injuries, etc. were obstacles and disabilities, but preparation, practice, talent, coaching prowess and team commitment all comprised the team's determination. Coach Calhoun's autograph could be under my signature of achievement (speaking of which it is a good thing my last name is Dodd instead of Consentinopapagopolous.

I think the reader sees the development here in order to achieve success, eleven major attributes are essential: vision, values, strength, mission, skills desires, motivation, purpose, direction, commitment, hard labor, and sweat. Please do not gloss over these words because they are the oxygen to keep your successful dream breathing. In hindsight, I had to learn these by experiences which did not always turn up rosy; I could have used this book a long, long time ago but it is never too late to learn and help others.

"There is no substitute for work. Worthwhile things come from hard work and careful planning."
-John Wooden

Key Chapter Points:

1: See your destination and then build your staircase to achieve it.

2: Success always worked best when I placed my destination first.

3: My signature for achievement has 4 components: disability, obstacles, determination and destination.

CHAPTER 8

"I'd hate to say my faith's a rock, but it's true. It is my strength; it gives me inner peace. Without my faith, I'd be in real bad shape. Faith gives a man hope and hope is what life is all about."

—Tom Landry

Throughout the previous seven chapters, you have noticed references to my faith peppered among my passages; peppering often refers to seasoning, which usually tends to be lightly sprinkled; my faith is one part of the most important triad of my life; my own well being (which includes spirituality) and the health, liveliness, and happiness of my immediate family, the deep rooted belief in my faith makes up the triad—collectively my "jumper cable". Remember Becky's favorite biblical verse, "I can do anything through Christ who gives me strength" (Philippians 4:13). Those ten words, deep in my heart and soul, are ten of the most important in my life. I believe that Jesus Christ has given each of his children talents to use as we live on earth. Deeply imbedded in my faith I must recognize the talents that God has bestowed upon me to put into use. If I chose not to use these talents, I would be failing both God and me. I would be a "rainbow in the dark," someone who has a gift that has been ignoring it. That is a lose/lose proposition for which I absolutely refuse to be associated with. Faith can be enigmatic at times. When one gets to the raw essence of faith, there is a surety for what one hopes (that is the easy part) yet there is an uncertainty on what one doesn't see (that's the thorny part). My hope is my goal and I plan to get there. The direction though (what is not seen) is the difficult corridor. Obviously, I know what I do see, but the future and the uncertainty is what can be worrisome. An analogous example is the Tour De France peleton when a group of cyclists breaks away from the lead pack and ventures into unknown terrain, and obstacles. The group believes in its training, skill and knowledge to achieve this breakaway, but a core of faith is present; it is its hope that this break-a-way will be successful.

Connection: Develop a plan to be your compass that directs you on your journey all the while keeping the destination in front of you.

The direction I am heading towards is well planned; I have set a mental road map which blends wisdom and guidance from family, friends, fellow church parishioners, church leaders, and business peers—especially those who have traveled the same pathway. They are the ones who felt the bumps along the road, suffered the bruises, and passed the warning tribulations to others to avoid the same hazards.

It is their experiences that I was looking for and learned from and passed on to others. So, with faith as my jumper cable power, my understanding delves the answers to six questions:

* Am I looking at direction through my eyes or through many eyes?

*Did I realistically consider possible disappointments, failures, and missed opportunities?

* Have I set up a contingency plan?

* Is there a realm or means of accountability?

* Did I plan for training and continuous learning?

* Do I have a confident, doubtful, or arrogant attitude?

The older I get, the more pronounced my faith becomes and the more thankful I am to the Lord. I have been blessed with good health, a very loving family, an amazing 35+ year career with one outstanding organization, and friendships that are very dear to me. Indeed, I am a very blessed and grateful man.

At this point, my paraphrased message to my readers is simple: "Get Up, Take Your Talents and Walk"! No person was placed on this planet earth to be a spectator—God has set a direction for each one of us; it is up to each of God's people to rise and get walking forward using the talents that have been placed in each one's realm. The key is to persevere and succeed despite challenges (something my father just was not able to grasp). For me, my backpack which I wear towards my goals in life, contains Truth, Righteousness, Morality, Decency, Readiness, Salvation, Spirit and an intertwinement of Faith that keeps these all linked together. On all occasions, my poignant prayer in the spirit is what keeps my jumper cables effective.

This might be the chapter that acts as a "turn off" to some. I may be judged as a religious Zealot, Bible Thumper, or "Jesus Freak." My jumper cables are wired and color coded by His word to be used correctly. I am deeply devoted to God and through his graciousness have lived a wonderfully full life with many unwritten chapters lying ahead. If you feel that you would like to self analyze where your goals and directions in life are, please keep reading. However, this book may not be for you; many people have not used God's jumper cables because of the lack of knowing, or knowing and disbelieving; no one forces you to use the power (talent) granted you by God. The power of choice is one asset that makes us higher than the animals.

"There is nothing in this world that can't be accomplished through hard work and with the help of God. Don't be afraid to talk to God; after all, He is our Father."
                              -Johnny Unitas

Key Chapter Points:

1:   *Faith in God, personal well being and health and happiness will always be the three most important aspects of my life.*

2:   *Ask yourself the series of questions above before starting on your success odyssey.*

3:   *Success does not come to those who are spectators—it must be strived for at full speed.*

CHAPTER 9

But those who trust in the Lord will find new strength.
They will soar high on wings like eagles.
They will run and not grow weary.
They will walk and not faint.

—Isaiah 40:29-31

I have heard it said and experienced that action is the only reality, and with that mentioned, the time for action (more specifically, YOUR action) has received its dinner invitation and is waiting for your reply. No more thinking about; no more wondering aloud; and emphatically, no more wishing that "this could be better if only . . . . It is time to take a pencil and construct **your signature of achievement**. It is the time to place your honest responses under the microscope with the core premise being, "How can I change my behavior for my own personal betterment?" This is the change that will prosper, will lead to success and in all likelihood, make you feel much better about yourself in life. Before you start listing answers on your "honest list," keep the following in your latent memory; they may be very helpful to you as they have for me:

*Remember God is strong and he wants you strong.

*Keep this thought. This is no afternoon athletic contest that we'll walk away from and forget about in a couple of hours. This is for keeps.

* Be prepared. You're up against far more than you can handle on your own. Take all the help you can get, every tool God has issued, so that when it's all over but the shouting, your "cables" have done the job.

* Learn to apply these distractions. Truth, righteousness, peace, faith and salvation are more than words. Learn how to apply them. You'll need them throughout life.

* Pray with sincerity and perseverance. God's Word is an indispensable weapon. In the same way, prayer is essential in the ongoing warfare. Pray for your brothers and sisters.

* Keep your eyes open and fixed on God.

* Fix your eyes on what you're doing; accept the hard times along with the good; keep the Message alive; do a thorough job as God's servant.

*Shout praise to our God. Depend on Him, He's an honest judge. He'll do right not only by me, but by everyone eager for his coming.

* Forget yourselves long enough to lend a helping hand. Don't push your way to the front; don't sweet-talk your way to the top. Put yourself aside, and help others get ahead. Don't be obsessed with getting your own advantage.

Start making an honest list in response to the following twenty insightful questions:

Where is my strength? What gives me energy? What are my reasons and motives to face each new day?

How can I take my stand? What trajectory will I follow to reach my desired destination?

Where is my point of focus? Am I distracted? What is diverting my attention from the gold medal?

What are my struggles? Remember, the best way to overcome obstacles is to initially recognize them!

What can I endure? Ask yourself what are the disturbances, the demons, the pain, and the uncomfortable encounters

that are dealt to you? Until these scoundrels are recognized, they can not be conquered.

For what purpose am I training? Be realistic and be specific. Don't just say, "I want a new job." Instead, say I want to be a head chef at a marquee restaurant in Chicago or I want to manage a housing project in downtown Columbus to help inner city families.

How should I plan and move forward? This is my playbook and mine alone. Make it orderly and with a timeline. "Someday" frequently translates to "No Day." For example, if it is a degree one is seeking, do six major promises:

1. I will set a graduation date (say, May, 2016)
2. I will sign up for two college classes this summer
3. I will take one or two classes each semester
4. I will complete all my homework and projects
5. I will study hard for my mid terms and finals
6. **I WILL GRADUATE AS I PLANNED!**

What should my attitude be? Without question, one can't control circumstances, but can control attitude. Make sure my attitude stays upbeat—no behavior was ever changed for the better with a sour, downtrodden attitude.

What are my sources of strength? God? Family? Friends? Pro Athletes? Only I will know what strengthens me and keep in mind that it may change over time.

Where is my foundation; do I have one? Similar to your sources of strength, what is the "wind beneath my wings?"

Keep this list true to your heart—it won't fail you . . .

And now it is time to have your signature of achievement harmoniously put into formation—to what are you going to hook your jumper cables? Where are you going to get a charge of power that transfers life from a wide awake battery to a sleepy one? Have you properly recognized

> **Connection: Identify your power source and connect your Jumper Cables to it. Begin your signature for achievement now!**

what obstacles may be obscuring your destination? What determination pathway are you going to launch to decimate these obstacles and reach your destination? Honest answers to these questions will be the only transitory flight to your goal. I hope I have delivered a "motivational zapping" to help inspire you, energize you and help you achieve success. Though this book may be at its finish line in terms of pages, in actuality, it is just the beginning for you to achieve your successful vision. Use the "jumper cables" God has provided and write a doable signature. I know each reader can succeed!

Good luck to you and never stop striving for greatness as we live and prosper in God's Kingdom.

I have fought the good fight, I have finished the race, I have kept the faith.
-Timothy: 4-7

Tim is a Certified Executive Coach (ACC) with the ICF (International Coach Federation) and holds a Professional Coach Certification (GPCC) from the Gestalt Institute, Cleveland, Ohio. The key areas of focus for Tim Dodd Executive Coaching & Consulting are:

- Facilitate professional growth and personal development toward improved performance.
- Assist others as they work towards specific professional goals—career transition, communication, performance management, organizational effectiveness, executive presence, enhancing strategic thinking, dealing effectively with conflict, and effective team building.
- Assist you in making a connection for change management, best practices, information and knowledge, developing plans for improvement
- Leadership development – creating and developing activity that enhances the quality of leadership within both the individual and organization
- Increasing leadership effectiveness via practice, focus, and persistence toward individual and group development as leaders
- Being as much about helping you drive profitability as about your personal development

In the role as Executive Coach, my desire is to help others in corporate arenas and individually understand where they are versus where they think they want to be in the following areas:

- Strategically (company focus—seeing the bigger picture both short and long term)
- Professionally (corporate role—performance, competence, career planning)
- Leadership Development (corporate roles - self and leadership teams)
- Personally (life balance—work / home / family / personal desires)

I will be a tool, catalyst, and influence to lead executives and their leadership team to begin and/or continue their journey to attain goals that they have for themselves and their organizations. Realizing that often, a goal may not be reached or attained—I want to help executives realize the journey and experiences along the way—successes and failures – are the journey. Together, lets *Generate Energy for Change and Growth!*

Contact Information:
Web page: http://executivecoachingandconsulting.com
Email: tim@executivecoachingandconsulting.com